To Whom Much Is Given

To Whom Much Is Given

How the Traverse City Rotary Club Responded

To Ross Child
Thanks for Awareness
Creating Taking Action

[signature]

Ronald W. Sondee
Rotary Club of Traverse City, Michigan
Traverse City, Michigan

2000 - 2001

Published by Rotary Club of Traverse City, Michigan
115 Park Avenue
Traverse City, Michigan 49684

Publisher's Cataloging-in-Publication Data
Sondee, Ronald W.
    To whom much is given: how the Traverse City Rotary Club
    responded / Ronald W. Sondee. -- Traverse City, MI: Traverse City
    Rotary Club, 2000.
        p.   ill.   cm.

    ISBN 0-9650497-0-1
        1. Rotary Club of Traverse City--History.
        2. Traverse City (Mich.)--History.   I. Title

HF5001.R82 T73   2000   00-104640
369.5/2   dc-21   CIP

PROJECT COORDINATION BY BOOKPUBLISHING.COM

03 02 01 00 • 5 4 3 2 1

Printed in the United States of America

CONTENTS

Appendices

FOREWORD

To Whom Much is Given is a fascinating story of the Traverse City Rotary Club during the 20th Century. The book has a special meaning for me for a number of reasons. I was a small boy when Rotary was founded by a group of dedicated local business and professional men, including my father, James T. Milliken, who became its first President. Those 24 founding members, and many who came after them, had a special enthusiasm and vision of what this area of the state was and could become. They knew that business and professional leaders, sharing ideas and resources, could have a major impact on improving the quality of life and opportunities for the youth and other members of our community.

I was privileged as a young Boy Scout to enjoy the beauty and opportunities of Camp Greilick, acquired and developed through the foresight of those early Rotarians. In the 1920s they saw the need for a youth camp where Boy Scouts, Girl Scouts and 4-H Club members could develop diverse skills and enjoy the beauties of nature. I will ever remember those happy days, summer after summer, at Camp Greilick.

As a young man I enjoyed working in the family's department store businesses in Traverse City and northern Michigan. And for many years I was an active and enthusiastic member of the Traverse City Rotary Club before embarking on a career in politics, first as a state senator, then lieutenant governor, and later serving as governor of Michigan for 14 years.

I was always proud of my roots being in the Grand Traverse region, and particularly of the accomplishments of the community, including those spearheaded or supported by the Traverse City Rotary Club.

The history of our region has always meant a great deal to me and to Helen. We have been extremely pleased with the historic renovations that have been made possible through Rotary's application of mineral revenues derived from the camp lands. Rotary has been able to support the preservation and restoration of such landmark treasures as the Traverse City Opera House, the Park Place Hotel, the Benzie Area Historical Museum, the Alden Railroad Museum, the State Theatre, the Con Foster Museum and many other projects.

Those of us who have lived in the Grand Traverse region know that we are blessed with one of the most beautiful natural areas in the world, with its lakes, rivers, streams, forests, and hills of incredible beauty. It is especially heartening to realize that monies received by Rotary from its lands have been invested to protect and preserve our land and waters through wise planning and conservation efforts. Creating the Grand Traverse Regional Land Conservancy, and continuing to support far-reaching conservation projects, is a prime example. We are grateful for the vision of Rotary members toward assuring that the beauty of our area will remain in perpetuity.

These kinds of dedicated efforts have been repeated over and over again since the beginning of the Traverse City Rotary Club over 80 years ago. Rotarians have made a major difference in the quality of all of our lives.

William G. Milliken
Governor of Michigan
1969-1983

ACKNOWLEDGMENTS

The following persons have made contributions of their talent, time and information toward the production of this book, all of which is gratefully acknowledged:

Jack Bay, Jack Broadfoot, Glen Chown, Bob Dean, Stacey Foster, Jeff Hickman, Gary Hogue, Leo Hughes, Wendell Johnson, Graham Keevil, Bill Kildee, Tamara Lubic, John McKinney, Wes Nelson, Olave Russell, Margaret Scott, Frank Sisson, Marsha Smith, Ben Taylor, Pat Wilson and Robert Yeiter.

Information was also derived from *The ABC's of Rotary*, by Cliff Dochterman, and the Rotary Foundation of Rotary International.

Photographs by Steve Largent, Dick Bolton, John Williams, Ted Cline, John Russell and the Grand Traverse Regional Land Conservancy are also deeply appreciated.

INTRODUCTION

This book is a project underwritten by Rotary Charities of Traverse City, Inc., whose Board of Trustees determined that it would be worthwhile to preserve some of the activities and history of the Traverse City Rotary Club during its first eighty years, from 1920 to 2000. Many members of our club have been queried in recent years by people throughout Michigan and other parts of the world regarding details of "the richest Rotary Club in the world," whether such designation was true, how it came about, and what we were doing with "all of that money." They have referred, of course, to the incredible good fortune of our Rotary Club owning land upon which reserves of oil and gas were discovered, wells were drilled and royalties have been received for over twenty years.

The undersigned, as a Rotary Charities Board member, was requested to chair a Rotary Book Committee. One of the basic tenets of Rotary is never to say no when asked to perform a particular task, so I dutifully accepted (not realizing the duty would evolve to writing most of the book). Other committee members were appointed, including Frank Sisson, Ben Taylor, Gary Hogue, Frank Stulen, Jack Bay and Bob Dean, sitting in as President of Rotary Charities. The

Committee determined that we did not want the book to concentrate only on our well-known revenues from oil and gas wells, which in itself is a unique story, but rather to encompass many of the dedicated efforts and accomplishments of the Club from its very beginning.

Bits and pieces of history and photographs were collected from many sources, and the Committee, as well as the Rotary Charities Board, discussed from time to time the appropriate scope and purpose of the book. After what seemed like an interminable period of compilation, writing and re-writing, the entire Board reviewed the manuscript and authorized publication of a hard-cover book. We hope that the time and effort of many persons will result in a worthwhile benefit for those reading these pages.

Ronald W. Sondee

IN THE BEGINNING

Chronicling an abbreviated history of the Rotary Club of Traverse City is an awesome task, since so much has been accomplished by so many outstanding persons over its 80-year life. It seems appropriate to do so, however, as its 20th Century existence concludes, and we look at the results we have achieved and the opportunities for accomplishing even more in the 21st Century.

The original Rotary Club was chartered in Chicago in 1905 by attorney Paul Harris and a small group of his business friends, who recognized an absence of fellowship and camaraderie among their peers in industry and the professions. They decided to form an association or club that would meet from week to week, rotating their meeting locations among the offices of the members. Thus the name "Rotary" came into being. The second, third, fourth and fifth clubs were chartered in 1908, in San Francisco, Oakland, California, Seattle and Los Angeles. By 1910 Detroit received the 16th charter, and also that year Winnipeg, Canada became the 35th club, making the organization international. This rapid national and international growth exploded throughout the 20th Century, to virtually all areas of the world.

Paul Harris was a frequent summer visitor to the Grand Traverse area, exhibiting his usual enthusiasm as an ambassador of good will and the principles of Rotarians providing needed services to their communities and eventually to the world, while employing the highest ethical standards in their businesses and professions.

In 1920, when Rotary was just 15 years old and consisted of over 700 clubs, a committee comprised of Grand Rapids Rotarians visited Traverse City to determine if the town was big enough to support a club of its own. By March 20 of that year, two dozen business and professional men with different "classifications" were enlisted as Charter Members, and a provisional Charter was granted. A permanent Charter, No. 754, was issued on May 1, 1920. The Club's first president was State Senator James Milliken, whose son, William (also a Traverse City Rotarian), would serve as Governor of Michigan from 1969 to 1983, longer than any other Governor in Michigan's history.

Since Rotary International now boasts more than 28,000 clubs worldwide, the Traverse City Club was truly a pioneer in the amazing growth of the international organization, as well as in the impressive growth of the Grand Traverse region. Among its early community projects, Rotarians were active in establishing the Traverse City Chamber of Commerce in 1921, the first five presidents being Rotarians. Over the years approximately two-thirds of the Chamber presidents have come from the Rotary Club.

Number 754

The International Association of Rotary Clubs

Hereby Certifies that the ROTARY CLUB of

Traverse City, Michigan

has been elected to membership in this Association and, having agreed to be bound by the Constitution thereof, which agreement is duly evidenced by the acceptance of this certificate, is declared to be an affiliating club of the International Association of Rotary Clubs, to be and remain such as provided by the Constitution of this Association.

Witness the seal of the International Association of Rotary Clubs, duly attested by its officers, this

first day of May Anno Domini 1920.
(This is a duplicate charter issued 11 December, 1946)

_____
President

_____
Secretary

ROTARY CAMPS FOR YOUTH

In 1923, the Club president was Clarence L. Greilick, an avid outdoorsman, who proposed an idea for one of the Club's earliest projects—the establishment of a community campground, to be used by the 4-H, Boy Scouts and Girl Scouts, each group having an allotted time for camp use. The membership approved the concept and raised $1100 to buy some 450 acres of land in the Spider Lake and Rennie Lake areas. That endeavor proved so successful that a very impressive $7500 was next raised to purchase an additional 27 acres of land. The new acreage had Rennie Lake frontage and gave the camp excellent facilities for water sports.

Control of the camp was turned over to a non-profit organization made up of representative Rotarians, to be named the Community Camp Association. Some 19 years later, then president, Jack Freethy, convinced the Club members that the property should be deeded back to an organization of the Club. Most of the 210 shares of stock which had been issued by the Community Camp Association were owned by individual Rotarians, many of whom had died. It was necessary to garner all available shares and sell enough additional stock to assure a favorable vote for the transfer. By 1955, all of the assets of the Community Camp Association had been turned over to a new non-profit corporation, Rotary Camps, Inc., with Rotary Club officers at the helm. This arrangement stayed in effect until 1977, when Rotary Camps, Inc. (later to be named Rotary Camps & Services of Traverse City, Inc.) was reorganized and began operating under a separate board of directors.

In 1955 Rotary Camps, Inc. leased the former Community Camp Association property, known as Camp Greilick, to the Scenic Trails Council Boy Scouts of America for 99 years, for the sum of one dollar, fortunately reserving mineral rights in the land. At one point the outright title to the property had been offered to the Boy Scouts, who declined the offer. The lease with the Boy Scouts was later converted to a trust agreement, preserving the essential provisions of the previous lease, with a term expiring in the year 2053.

Boy Scouts' Camp Greilick entrance.

Boy Scouts' Camp Greilick waterfront.

By that time it was the growing Girl Scouts organization which needed major assistance. With Traverse City as its regional headquarters, the Girl Scouts had been splitting the summer schedule with the boys at Camp Greilick. With enrollment rapidly growing in both organizations, the Girl Scouts needed a summer camp of their own. Frank Power, local physician, was chairman of Rotary Camps and together with his wife, Margo Power, spearheaded the effort to provide separate land for the use of the Girl Scouts. A committee was formed to survey the area by air and to begin research into land titles. Rotary Camps bought acreage on Bass Lake, southwest of Traverse City, and began building lodge and tent foundations. This property became known as Camp Sakakawea, and its 393.5 acres were leased to the Crooked Tree Girl Scout Council in 1956 for 15 years, which lease was amended (and later converted to a trust agreement) extending the term to May 31, 2002. In the ensuing years the Traverse City Rotary Club and the Rotary Camps organization continued to support the

Camp Sakakawea entrance - 1970

Camp Sakakawea waterfront - 1970

capital needs of both camps, primarily through the Good Works Fund of the Club.

During these decades of acquiring land for providing services to youth, little did the Rotary leaders realize that the income to be subsequently derived from some of that land would give Club members the opportunity to put their motto, "Service Above Self," to perhaps the highest level in the world of Rotary. That good fortune is described below, as it unfolded in the 1960's and 1970's.

COMMITTEE FOR THE HANDICAPPED — TAG DAY

Helping handicapped individuals is another example of how the Rotary Club, from its earliest days, has been instilled with a will to serve in nearly every walk of community life. No sooner had one project been up and running than another one was found. From 1935 through 1981 the Club was a primary sponsor of the Grand Traverse Chapter of the Easter Seal Society for Crippled Children and Adults, which role included countless hours by Rotarians and wives stuffing Easter Seal appeal envelopes. In 1982 the Club withdrew from its affiliation with the Easter Seal Society in order to apply all raised funds directly to the beneficiaries, and reorganized its efforts as the Rotary Committee for the Handicapped. To raise funds, Tag Day was initiated, with Rotarians gathering at a specified meeting place throughout a Saturday in June, donning Rotary aprons, putting on Rotary caps, picking up Rotary pails, a couple of fistfuls of Rotary thank you tags and heading out to prescribed high traffic locations for two-hour stints, applying their incomparable Rotary persuasion to a generously responding public. The first Tag Day generated $5,000 in funds. Now more than $21,000 is raised each year on this one day, with the contributions being augmented through matching challenge grants. In addition, the specialized talents of Rotary members have been applied to the needs of the handicapped, with doctors and dentists in particular being generous with donated time and services.

As a result, deformed teeth are repaired, so that a child is happy to smile again; a student with cerebral palsy now has a voice activated computer; special equipment is provided to the hearing impaired so they can type telephone messages to doctors' offices and others, receiving valuable written responses; a van was purchased and modified for a severely handicapped student, who now transports himself and gives motivational talks to other disabled persons; a matching grant was given for community assisted living apartments; and such equipment as wheelchairs and a mechanized chair lift for putting handicapped persons in and out of the Civic Center pool have been provided.

One example was reported by the Traverse City Record-Eagle in 1997, concerning a fifteen-year-old girl confined to a wheelchair because of a rare, life-threatening disease that caused internal bleeding in her legs. For two years she had been unable to attend classes at school, or do much else that involved leaving the house. When alerted to the situation, the Committee for the Handicapped approved the purchase of a $2200 desktop computer system, which enabled the student to keep up with her schoolwork over the Internet. This money came from quarters and dollars raised by individual Rotarians on Tag Day.

The driving, agitating, relentless force behind these individual efforts has been Jim Beckett, Chairman of the Committee for the Handicapped for over thirty years. His boundless enthusiasm and perseverance has exemplified the best of what dedicated Rotarians can accomplish.

Jim Beckett licking his chops while collecting another Tag Day donation.

WHEN THE SAINTS GO MARCHING IN

In 1942, although the Club was involved in a number of annual projects, there was a feeling on the part of some that too many members were settling back in their personal participation, treating Rotary as a luncheon club, full of good will but short on activities. Once again, a leadership group began discussing new ideas for raising money, boosting attendance at meetings, and rekindling the spirit of Rotary. It was then that an inspired team of younger members proposed a Minstrel Show. Such shows had been performed for years across the country, blending music with good-hearted humor. As plans for such a show began to emerge, some of the more elderly Rotarians were astounded at the crazy antics being proposed by the core group, and were extremely skeptical that the show could raise the initial projected goal of $500.

The first show was held on two evenings at the old Lyric Theater (now the State Theater) and was performed in black-face, as had been done traditionally elsewhere for many years. That initial show was a financial success, netting the grand sum of $507. This was enough money to pay for a new well at the scout camp, which some of the younger members drove by hand, pulling a rope with weights to drive the pipe. The show was now off and running, and grew to be a much anticipated annual event. The instigation and success of the early shows have been credited in large measure to the leadership of Doug Linder as Master of Ceremonies, Jack Freethy, Hal Jordan and John Minnema. Jack Freethy was music director and piano player, and several years later was joined by the first Pit Band, comprised of a saxophone, banjo, bass and drums. Many years later Doug Linder was interviewed concerning those early shows, and reminisced as follows: "When you dig into hometown talent, you can usually find many capable, very talented people, especially it seems in the Traverse City area. Over the years we had a tremendous amount of sheer fun. We had a good time putting on a Minstrel Show, and a lot of people left laughing."

The success of the show became known throughout northern Michigan, resulting in invitations to perform extra shows in Manistee, Cheboygan and Boyne City for a number of years.

After a few years of traditional "minstrel" routines, the show was boosted to a new level of performance in 1949 by the addition of Bill Kildee and Wally Campbell, a local comedy duo, who were not then members of Rotary. Their act became known as "Willy and Wally" and was so hilarious and well-received that it went on to gain national attention. In 1977 they were invited to perform before the Saints and Sinners Club for a "Roast" of Traverse City's own U.S. Senator Robert Griffin at the Shoreham Hotel in Washington D.C. They shared the spotlight with Hubert Humphrey, a close friend of Senator Bob, the Senate Minority Leader. A delegation of local Rotarians joined them at the event. Willy and Wally's talented acts and writing of many skits for others inspired their fellow Rotarians into a faster-paced, more topical show, adding a greater variety of acts, such as comedy cross-overs.

The black-face make-up was eliminated in the 1960's, in response to racial sensitivity. The show's performers next

Willy and Wally's famous "Cocktails for Two" - 1975

wore white clown faces for several years, before baring their own facial anomalies, with light make-up ever since. Eventually the word "minstrel" was dropped, and it became simply the Rotary Show.

There has been no let down in over a half century of production. The performers have been primarily amateurs drawn from the area (mostly Rotarians, who epitomized the word "amateur"). But the Rotary Club has also been blessed over the years with highly talented members, including professionals in the fields of music, writing, directing and conducting. To attempt to list even the most talented contributors would risk excluding so many others. Suffice it to say that the show over the years has been led by a cadre of normally serious Rotarian men and women, whose zaniness blossoms each spring into a show that not only raises large amounts of money for its Good Works purposes, but also draws positive reviews from all but the most observant critics. Some of the acts are spectacular, particularly when individuals from the Interlochen

Center for the Arts and other local schools are recruited to spotlight special talents. Some of the funniest moments are those when the performers forget their lines, and the audience wills them back into place by laughter and applause. Annual highlights of the show are those skits and jokes poking fun at local leaders and businesses—quite often performed by those self-same leaders and business men and women. "It is an unusual spectacle for our little town to have prominent men and women on stage making fools of themselves," stated one of the present day prime movers of the show. "It's three months or more of preparation, plus rehearsals and a four-night show. We make a lot of money, but in reality the Rotary Show is the glue holding the Club together and reminds the community of our roots."

A major element and tradition of the show is to strive for nearly one hundred percent participation from the Club members, who year after year are involved in producing, writing and arranging the music and acts, assembling and writing a comprehensive program book replete with cartoons and spoofs on members' businesses, selling ads for the program book, directing music and "production" acts, singing in the chorus, participating in skits and "news reporting," selling popcorn, pop and programs, participating in the pre-show audience participation activities, working on the stage, lighting and sound crews, and other onstage or offstage performance. It is certainly a total Club endeavor, with a huge commitment of time and energy over several months each year.

The results of all that energy and wit are certainly worthwhile. From that initial $507 raised in the 1942 show, the net proceeds have risen to over $70,000 each year, all of which are placed in the Club's Good Works Fund. Contributions from the fund have gone to Boy and Girl Scout Councils, the City Opera House, the Traverse City Symphony Orchestra, Special Olympics, Hospices, the Salvation Army, projects dealing with literacy and child care in the community, and the Traverse City Public and Catholic Schools, to name only a few of the recipients.

Perhaps there is just a bit of appropriate connection to that song with which the Rotary Chorus and Pit Band begin every performance, with the singers marching down the aisles of the auditorium and onto the stage—*When The Saints Go Marching In!*

Chorus Director Ken Jewell of Interlochen fame leads singers in Silver Anniversary Show in 1967.

BLACK GOLD!!

Although enthusiasm and hard work may beget good fortune, it was a stroke of very good luck that allowed the Rotary Club to expand its charitable services to a level never dreamed of by those wise early members who bought the land for youth camps. The first thoughts of oil and gas development on Rotary lands south of town began stirring in 1967, when Rotary Camps, Inc. and Consumers Power Company agreed to a five-year lease of Camp Greilick for potential mineral exploration. However, Consumers Power (and this must have given it some abdominal gas over the ensuing years) let the lease expire without exercising its rights.

A further stroke of good fortune (or more appropriately, wise delegation of Rotary talent) for the Club and community occurred in 1975, when negotiations for a new mineral lease were assigned to four astute members, attorney Al Arnold, Dr. Frank Power, Jerry McCarthy, and Bob Hilty. This Rotary team extracted a spectacular deal with lessee A. G. Hill, providing the Club with royalties of 25 percent until all production costs were met, and 40 per cent thereafter! This was a very unusual contract, forgoing the payment of royalties up front for a much larger return if oil and gas were found. The rest is history. The following year, while the country was celebrating its 200th birthday, we hit paydirt! However, no drilling was to be allowed near any of the camp buildings, the drilling noises had to be muffled, and the integrity of the camping facility was maintained. Six wells eventually came in, and the Rotary Club was faced with how to handle this bonanza in a way that would best serve the community, and at the same time preserve the charitable activities of the Rotary Club, which could have been negatively impacted by this sudden influx of dollars. In addition, the leadership needed to find a way to shelter oil and gas income from taxes, in order to make more resources available to the community.

With this newly found wealth, and visions of much more to come, there were as many ideas of what to do with the money as there were members of the Club. One thought could easily have been that money-raising ventures by the Club would no longer be needed. Why bother continuing to ring those Salvation Army bells? Why give up weekend hours to raise money on Tag Day? Why pester fellow businessmen to buy ads in the annual Rotary Show program? Why bother putting on a show at all? Much more money than was produced by all of these projects combined would now be available without anyone lifting a finger.

The downside, of course, could have been that the Traverse City Rotary Club, as a service organization, would turn into a Rotary Luncheon Club, and its original purposes forgotten. Then President-Elect Bill Kildee proposed creating a local charitable foundation to control the oil and gas revenues. Jack Bensley, another of the Club's leaders, told the members: "We are going to structure this thing so that you guys can never get to it. You will still have to raise your own money for good works." No other course of action was ever contemplated.

Rotary Camp's first well drilling toward paydirt in February, 1976.

ROTARY CHARITIES OF TRAVERSE CITY, INC.

In 1977 the first oil and gas royalties were received, and soon thereafter an historic decision was made. It was determined that mineral revenues would be separated from normal Rotary activities by the establishment of two tax-exempt organizations: "Rotary Camps & Services, Inc.," which would hold title to the land, and "Rotary Charities of Traverse City, Inc.," which would receive and administer all of the oil and gas revenues. This was done in a giant leap of faith, with no assurance that the federal government would grant tax-exempt status. A year would pass before the Internal Revenue Service gave its final approval. In fact, Rotary Camps, Inc. had already received initial payments of oil and gas revenues, but held them in escrow until the new Rotary Charities of Traverse City was organized. To further protect the fund, it was decided early on that the oil and gas revenues would comprise the corpus of the fund, and that only a portion of the earnings from the fund would be used for charitable grant-making. As a result of this mandate, the corpus of the fund has grown impressively over the years, currently over $40 million and steadily rising, hopefully with continued strong investment performance and vigilant management.

In an effort to establish a proper organization to meet

the requirements of the IRS for tax exemption, the leadership called on help from the National Council of Foundations and asked its Executive Director to come to Traverse City for consultation. Not only was the allure of helping shape a new charitable foundation here, but the Executive Director had a strong interest in birds and heard that the Kirtland Warbler was in the area. He reportedly relished the prospect of seeing this rare bird. History does not record whether the Warbler obliged. Ultimately a recommendation was developed, with the assistance of legal experts, that the new organization obtain public charity status as a "tax-exempt supporting organization" of the Rotary Club of Traverse City. Arrival of the IRS tax exemption letter dated June 23, 1978 marked the real beginning of a charitable giving program unprecedented in northern Michigan.

The Articles of Incorporation of Rotary Charities of Traverse City, Inc. provide that the corporation "is organized

Some of the members of the first Rotary Charities Board of Directors in August, 1976, standing in front of Rotary Camps well no.1. Left to Right: Dr. Frank Power, Bruce Needham, Graham Keevil, Bill Kildee, Doug Linder, Art Huey, Pete Strom and Jack Bensley.

and shall be operated exclusively for charitable, scientific, literary and educational purposes, by making gifts, grants and distributions to and which exclusively benefit" such organizations. The corporate By-Laws add that such grants include "contributions or gifts to a state or any political subdivision thereof, but only if the contribution or gift is made for exclusively public purposes," and to "corporations, trusts, community chests, funds or foundations organized and operated exclusively for charitable, scientific, literary or educational purposes . . ." The charitable purpose restrictions of the Internal Revenue Code have been meticulously followed by the Rotary Charities Board from its inception.

The purposes and geographic area to be served by Rotary Charities are further described in its "Mission Statement":

> **The Mission of Rotary Charities of Traverse City is to provide appropriate funding, within its resources, to organizations primarily within the five-county Grand Traverse area in order to improve the well-being of the area with special emphasis on youth, community needs and quality of life. The five priority areas for grant-making are: affordable housing, education, environment/managing growth, culture/recreation and strengthening families."**

This Mission Statement is part of the Strategic Plan of Rotary Charities, as revised in 1998. The five-county area served includes Grand Traverse, Leelanau, Antrim, Kalkaska, and Benzie Counties.

The corporate members of Rotary Charities are comprised of the entire membership in good standing of the Rotary Club of Traverse City. Such members elect the Charities Board of Trustees, consisting of ten members, one of whom is the

President of the Rotary Club ex officio. Since its beginning in 1977, the Charities Board has been driven in its grant decisions by the basic principles of serving the diverse needs of our region and helping to improve the quality of life for all its residents. Since the first grants were given, Charities has been dedicated to helping people help themselves; providing educational, recreational and cultural facilities for public use; protecting our natural resources; strengthening our community's public and non-profit infrastructure; and enhancing the lives of young people and their families. In its more than 20 years of existence, Rotary Charities has given over 400 grants to nearly 200 charitable and governmental organizations, totaling over $29 million. Culture and recreation, economic development, education and health-related grants have accounted for more than 80 percent of the monies granted, most of these being in the "bricks and mortar" categories. Other categories receiving substantial grants include community and non-profit organizations development, the environment, strengthening youth and families, affordable housing and Rotary International projects.

Rotarian Les Biederman, who built Traverse City's first radio station and later its first television station, had been diagnosed with an advanced stage of cancer, and with inadequate treatment available locally, had to make frequent and exhausting trips to the University of Michigan Medical Center in Ann Arbor. Les pulled a switch on Rotary Charities by challenging it to match his $500,000 pledge to fund the establishment of a local cancer treatment center with a linear accelerator, now known as the Biederman Cancer Treatment Center at Munson Medical Center. Thus began the concept of "challenge grants" with Rotary Charities, although usually Charities has challenged recipients to match monies offered by Charities, thereby expanding philanthropy throughout the region.

The Dennos Museum at Northwestern Michigan College benefitted from Rotary Charities grants of $500,000 initially

Biederman Cancer Treatment Center, a collaboration of Les Biederman, Rotary Charities and Munson Medical Center.

and an additional $450,000 later on. This beautiful museum, sponsored in large part by Rotarian Mike Dennos and his wife Barbara, has seven galleries, an extensive collection of early and current art pieces and the Milliken Auditorium for Performing Arts. Both the Dennos Museum and the Cancer Center grants were used to prime the pump to raise much larger amounts in the community for these projects. That philosophy has prevailed in many of the grants made over the years.

It was during its second decade that Rotary Charities embarked on one of its biggest challenges, the purchase and renovation of the Park Place Hotel. This historic site, a Traverse City landmark for more than 100 years, had suffered through several ownerships and fallen into such disrepair that it was bankrupt and in danger either of becoming a boarded-up eyesore or of being put to a use not conducive to the viability or growth of downtown Traverse City. Either event could have had a disastrous effect on the City's core area, especially with the imminent construction of the Grand Traverse Mall adding

Dennos Museum at Northwestern Michigan College.

a million plus square feet of retail space south of town. Several club leaders and the Rotary Charities Board developed a vision of purchasing the hotel, refurbishing it and, in conjunction with Northwestern Michigan College, developing an educational facility to provide training for students in restaurant and hospitality programs. An additional key goal was to provide an anchor for downtown revitalization. A focus group of Rotarians toured the hotel and analyzed the financial aspects of acquisition and renovation within a very limited time frame, since the bankruptcy sale of the hotel was close at hand. While there were diverse views among Rotarians as to the wisdom of this undertaking, on August 2, 1989, at the bankruptcy auction held in Chicago, Rotary made the successful bid of just over $2 million, using a special grant from Charities, and suddenly the Rotary Club was in the hotel business. It was determined that Rotary Camps & Services would become the sponsor of a new charitable organization, "Rotary Center, Inc." This new entity was structured to meet IRS requirements as a grant recipient and was given the flexibility to own and operate a hotel and restaurant as a working laboratory, and pursuant to an educational agreement with Northwestern Michigan College, to create a hospitality education and training program. Because of the widespread need for such skills in our tourist area, it seemed a logical fit.

To restore the Park Place to its historic past, with modern rooms and facilities, the hotel was closed, work was commenced, and many costly surprises were discovered before it reopened with a gala party the evening of July 1, 1991. From the beginning of this endeavor, the Rotary Charities Board believed that once the renovation was complete and the operation of the hotel was again on a sound footing, a new quali-

Ribbon-cutting ceremony at grand reopening of the Park Place in the summer of 1991. Left to right: Leon Michael, Jim Tompkins, Dr. Don Good, John Goense, Gary Columbus, Art Elliot, Bruce Rogers and Jack Burns.

fied owner had to be found who would continue the operation of the hotel as a major downtown asset well into the 21st Century. Although even more grants for operation had to be approved by Charities before an acceptable buyer was found, a sale was finally consummated in May, 1996 to Regency Traverse City Hotel Ventures, owned by a Minnesota group operating 38 hotels and restaurants in 12 states. As a condition of the sale, the new owner committed to additional substantial investment in the hotel, and made a "best efforts" commitment to continue the educational mission.

Rotary Center, Inc. could now be dissolved. Despite the difficult and costly stages of this unusual undertaking, Rotarians and others note that the downtown area is now flourishing more strongly than ever, and a beautiful and successful Park Place Hotel continues to breathe life into the center of our City.

Park Place Hotel in downtown Traverse City, after renovation.

A series of substantial Rotary Charities grants has also been given to the historic Traverse City Opera House, another downtown treasure desperately needing renovation and preservation. The Opera House, although still going through stages of improvement and expansion, now continues to host many civic functions, music, dramatic and educational programs, just as it did during the lumbering era of the late 1800's.

Traverse City Opera House.

In a similar vein, and adding further revitalization to downtown Traverse City, a challenge grant of $1 million was approved by Charities to renovate and expand the State Theater, so that it can become a home for the Traverse Symphony Orchestra, and a venue for major professional and amateur musical and dramatic productions, including local and touring companies. In addition, it will provide educational and performing opportunities for aspiring young people in the Grand Traverse region.

Major grants have also been awarded over the years to the Northwestern Michigan College University Center (unique in

Michigan), the Women's Center at Munson Medical Center, Between The Fences project at Thirlby/Running Field, Grand Traverse Area Catholic Schools' capital campaign, United Way of Northwestern Michigan, Scenic Trails Boy Scout Council, Crooked Tree Girl Scout Council, Twin Lakes 4-H Camp, Traverse City Christian School, Grand Traverse Bay YMCA, Old Town Playhouse, Clinch Park Zoo and Munson Medical Center's Hospitality House.

The predominantly bricks and mortar projects tell only part of the story, however. Perhaps an even greater difference Rotary Charities has made and will make may be measured only in the future, when the impact of our long-term investments in the organizations and social infrastructure of the area can be evaluated. Long-term strategic grant-making can best be illustrated in the organizations and projects Charities has "incubated": The Grand Traverse Regional Land Conservancy, which since its beginning in 1991 has become one of the largest land trust organizations in the state, now protecting in perpetuity over 8700 acres of critical land and over 25 miles of water frontage on lakes, rivers and streams; The Grand Traverse Regional Community Foundation, organized in 1992 with major Charities support to provide a vehicle for individuals and organizations to build endowments, now totaling over $17,000,000 in 175 funds, the income from which supports a wide variety of programs and community needs; HomeStretch, a regional Community Development Corporation specializing in providing affordable housing; T.A.R.T. Trails, Inc., a regional recreational trail organization; and the initiation by Charities of the Quality of Life Index, a project coordinated by the Grand Traverse Regional Community Foundation, Northwestern Michigan College and Michigan State University Extension to provide a reference for the five-county region to evaluate strengths, weaknesses and priority issues. Grant-making preference is given by Charities to those projects that utilize the Quality of

Life Index to evaluate progress in the problem areas being addressed.

The Pyatt Lake Nature Preserve on Old Mission Peninsula was the first land acquisition project of the Grand Traverse Regional Land Conservancy, founded by Rotary in 1991.

These far-reaching organizations have developed into partners with Rotary Charities, working together to meet the challenges of our region's growing communities, with established goals of well-planned land use and preservation, increased and leveraged charitable giving, innovative housing programs, development of ever-expanding outdoor trails, and preservation and access to rivers, lakes, quiet areas and other recreational amenities. Many of these incubation projects were spawned and developed through the leadership of Rob Collier, who was the first professional Executive Director of Rotary Charities, serving from 1989 to 1995. He is now President of the prestigious Council of Michigan Foundations.

Rotary Charities grants have also been widely dispersed throughout our five-county area. Youth and adult sports facilities have been built or expanded through grants for the Bellaire athletic fields, Mancelona all-weather track and field construction, Buckley athletic fields, Kalkaska Public Schools athletic facilities, Kalkaska Sports Complex Authority, Kalkaska Village Chalker Park, Leelanau Park's soccer field, Elberta Waterfront Community Playground, Betsie Valley Trail, Leelanau Trails Association, Glen Arbor tennis courts, Leland Public Schools multi-purpose court construction, Suttons Bay youth sports facilities, Traverse City Area Public Schools track complex, Kingsley athletic field improvements, Hickory Hills Ski Area projects, athletic complex at Elk Rapids High School, Central Lake Community Recreation, Mayfield Pond Park, North American VASA, Inc., Traverse Bay Area Youth Soccer fields, Grand Traverse Area Skateboard Park, Grand Traverse County Multi-Purpose Arena facility, and the list goes on and on.

In the realm of education, arts and culture, in addition to those already described, substantial grants have gone to Northwestern Michigan College, Northport Community Arts Center, Interlochen Center for the Arts, WIAA Public Radio, Traverse Symphony Orchestra, Inland Seas Education Association, Traverse Bay Area Intermediate School District, Traverse City Area Public Schools, Kingsley Area Public Schools, Benzie County Central Schools, Mancelona Schools, Green Lake Township Library, Bellaire Public Library, Elk Rapids District Library, Traverse Area District Library, Glen Lake Community Library and Suttons Bay Area District Library, among many others. Likewise, grants to museums and historical societies include the Benzie Area Historical Society,

Leelanau Historical Museum, Music House Museum, Bingham School Restoration, Helena Township's C&O Depot project, Con Foster Museum and others.

Support for the physical and mental health of the region has already been reflected in a number of the above-described major projects. In addition, many other health concerns have been investigated and grants awarded to such recipients as the Mancelona Area Health Clinic, the Grand Traverse Pavilions for their Intergenerational Community Center and Satellite Television System, Paul Oliver Memorial Hospital for emergency room and other improvements, Munson HealthCare's Advanced Life Support Services, the Benzie County Medical Care Facility, the American Red Cross for its new blood processing center, Northwest Michigan Blood Program's Mobile Drawing Unit, Manistee-Benzie Community Mental Health, Grand Traverse County Health Department's immunization outreach and dental clinic, the Michigan AIDS Fund and HIV/AIDS Wellness Networks, to name some additional such grantees.

From its earliest days, Rotary Charities has been deeply concerned with assisting family, youth and other human service needs. Meaningful impact has been attained with grants to Grand Traverse Families in Action, Northwest Michigan Child Guidance Clinic, the Salvation Army's Youth Latch Key program, Women's Resource Center for the renovation of a shelter home and a new emergency shelter, the Third Level Crisis Intervention Center for its new facility, Catholic Human Services, Inc., Child and Family Services of Northwest Michigan for child abuse prevention and for new facilities, Big Brothers Big Sisters of Northwestern Michigan, Boys and Girls Club of Grand Traverse, Northwest Michigan Council of Governments for its Kids First abuse prevention project, and Junior Achievement of Northwest Michigan. Pre-school, Head Start and child day-care programs have been the recipients of grants in Antrim, Benzie, Leelanau and Grand Traverse Counties. Adult and senior-care programs have also been supported in diverse locations, including assisting renovation of the Traverse City Senior Center and the Suttons Bay-Bingham Senior Friendship Community Center.

The GivEm' 40 Coalition is a community based partnership with United Way of Northwestern Michigan, the Grand Traverse Regional Community Foundation and Michigan State University, which focuses on positive "asset" development for at-risk children, helping to provide building blocks needed to succeed in life. Rotary Charities grants have helped initiate this program in 19 school districts throughout the 5 counties.

Low-cost housing and shelter projects have been supported with grants to Habitat for Humanity of the Grand Traverse Region, Antrim County Habitat for Humanity, HomeStretch, Good Samaritan Emergency Lodge and other projects in Antrim, Benzie, Kalkaska and Grand Traverse Counties. Vocational rehabilitation has been recognized in other projects, with grants to Antrim-Kalkaska Industries (Asgard building program) and GTP Industries in Grand Traverse County.

Other environmental and land planning programs receiving significant grants include the Jordan River Valley and Grass River Natural Area in Antrim County, the Leelanau Conservancy, the Boardman River Valley restoration and protection, Tip of the Mitt Watershed in Antrim County, Crystal Lake Watershed in Benzie County, Grand Traverse Bay Management Plan and Watershed Initiative, Northwest Michigan Council of Government's Zoning Reclassification Project, and numerous other land planning and conservancy projects.

Every one of these grants over more than 20 years has been extensively investigated by committees typically comprised of one Charities Board member and two or more Rotary members-at-large, who usually travel to the proposed project sites throughout the five counties. After recommendation is made by each Committee, extended discussion follows at a meeting of Charities Board members and other committee members during both the spring and fall grant cycles, at which time each proposed project is evaluated. Thereafter, the Charities Board meets and approves the final grants, based upon merit and available funds. $1 million to $2 million per year is disbursed in this meticulous manner, usually to approximately half of the applicants. Great emphasis has been placed by the investigation teams and Board on the capabilities of the applicants, the demonstrated need in their respective communities, and the process for implementation and evaluation that must be in place.

Although the Rotary Club of Traverse City has been incredibly fortunate to have gained access to the wealth produced from its land, enormous effort and time have been expended by its members to convert that good fortune toward the betterment of our area's citizens. Rotary Charities was well conceived and has borne fruit throughout our beautiful region.

ROTARY CAMPS & SERVICES, INC.

The predecessor organization of Rotary Camps & Services was Rotary Camps, Inc., described to some degree above under Rotary Camps for Youth. Rotary Camps was incorporated December 31, 1954 for the purpose of owning, operating and maintaining camps for the recreation, education and general health of youth, as well as for other more general charitable purposes. Rotary Camps became the titleholder to the Camp Greilick property in 1955. The discovery of oil and gas on that property necessitated, for tax reasons, the severance of the mineral interest from the primary title, with conveyance of the mineral interest to the new Rotary Charities entity in 1977.

Rotary Camps continued to hold title to the land, and ultimately determined that it should expand its purposes. In 1985, Rotary Camps amended its Articles of Incorporation to, among other things, expand the name of the organization from Rotary Camps to Rotary Camps & Services, Inc., and by adding the following principles to the purpose clause of its Articles:

1. Permit the holdings of Camp properties in trust;
2. Provide for the ownership, operation or holding outright or in trust of other non-profit community facilities;

3. Confirmation that Rotary Camps & Services had the power to make gifts and grants to other charitable organizations;
4. Confirmation that the organization would henceforth operate as a "supporting organization under Section 509 (a)(3) of the Internal Revenue Code."

Upon the approval of its restated Articles of Incorporation, Rotary Camps & Services applied for and obtained a tax exemption from the Internal Revenue Service in July 1985. Consequently, Camps & Services became the organization that enabled various other charitable activities, including serving as a qualified conservation entity capable of accepting conservation easements and/or conservation properties (until such time as the new Grand Traverse Regional Land Conservancy became qualified to act in that capacity) and to receive grants of real estate, specifically the Kalkaska Flowing Well Trout Farm (subsequently sold) and the Howard and Mary Edwards Preserve.

The Mission Statement of Camps & Services was adopted in 1998 as follows:

"To enhance the well-being of the five-county Grand Traverse Region by providing resources and forming pro-active, collaborative partnerships in the areas of affordable housing, recreation and land preservation."

Several years ago Howard Edwards, in memory of his wife, Mary Edwards, donated by will to Rotary Camps 720 acres of land in Paradise Township and another 40 acres in East Bay Township, designed to become the Howard and Mary Edwards Preserve. The Mission Statement adopted for the land provides in part: ". . .Rotary will manage the property to protect, enhance and promote public recreation, water quality, wildlife habitat, and ecological diversity in the Boardman River Valley so that the property remains an important and invaluable community resource." East Creek, a major tributary to the Boardman River, flows through the heart of this extensive tract of land, which is also vitally important as a wildlife and recreational link to state land and the Brown Bridge Quiet Area. To ensure prudent stewardship of this valuable resource, Camps & Services provided a $10,000 grant to the Grand Traverse Conservation District to prepare a comprehensive resource-based management plan for the property. This management

East Creek, in the heart of the Howard and Mary Edwards Preserve.

plan is to be integrated with other plans for the area, including Paradise and East Bay Township Master Plans, Grand Traverse County Master Plan, Brown Bridge Quiet Area Management Plan, Michigan Department of Natural Resources Traverse City Management Unit Forest Management Plan, Grand Traverse County Recreation Plan, and greenways and transportation plans. The management plan for the Edwards Preserve will include recommendations for hunting and trapping, timber harvest alternatives, oil and gas exploration, stream and habitat improvements, managing transportation issues and future development and re-routing of recreational trails.

Camps & Services acts as the Rotary arm or liaison for the Boy Scout and Girl Scout camps, as well as for the Edwards property. As such, Camps & Services oversees close to 2,000 acres of land. It also facilitates forestry contracts for harvesting of lumber on portions of those premises.

Camps & Services, in cooperation with Rotary Charities, also acts as the investigator and grant review committee for Boy Scout and Girl Scout capital needs at camp properties.

Charities and Camps & Services together have addressed another priority initiative for the region—affordable housing. Charities provided an $80,000 organizational capacity grant for HomeStretch, a community development corporation, and Camps & Services provided a loan guarantee of $200,000 to establish a revolving loan fund for property acquisition and pre-development startup costs. These funds were leveraged with state and federal dollars, building resources to help meet the critical need for housing that is affordable for working families.

ROTARY CLUB AND DISTRICT ORGANIZATION

In addition to its officers and board of directors, the activities of the Rotary Club are divided among numerous committees, each having major responsibilities. These committees include Club Service (including such sub-committees as Public Relations, Membership, Club Bulletin, Fellowship Activities and Music, to name a few); Community Service (including its sub-committees for the Handicapped, Youth, Community Events and Christmas Basket Program); International Service (including its sub-committees of Rotary Foundation, Student Exchange, Summer Youth Exchange, Group Study Exchange, World Community and Service Above Self); Rotary Show Committee; Budget and Audit Committee; Good Works Committee; Christmas Committee; Program Committee; STRIVE Committee; and other sub-committees as needed from time to time.

Officers and directors are elected at the annual meeting, and there are also annual meetings for Rotary Charities and Rotary Camps & Services, at which their respective boards of trustees are elected.

The Rotary Club of Traverse City is a member club of District 6290 of Rotary International, with 57 member clubs stretching from Holland and Grand Rapids in the south to

Wawa, Sault Ste. Marie and Blind River in Ontario, Canada. Even within our District, we are truly an international Club. Traverse City Rotary members have been very active in District activities over the years, holding many committee positions, hosting the District Convention, and having 5 members as Past District Governors.

Over its history the Traverse City Club, with something akin to a missionary spirit, sponsored or assisted in the organization of at least eight new clubs in northern Michigan. The Club was instrumental or assisted in organizing Rotary Clubs in Petoskey and Cheboygan in 1921 and Boyne City in 1922, and chartered Frankfort and Manistee in 1924, Suttons Bay in 1946, Elk Rapids in 1950 and Traverse City Sunrise Club in 1999. No other club in our District has as many charters to its credit. Having experienced the opportunities and satisfaction of Rotary membership over the years, the natural impulse of the Club was to help leaders in other communities provide service to others, while enjoying the camaraderie of participation.

INTERNATIONAL SERVICE AND WORLD FELLOWSHIP

One of the four basic objects of Rotary International is: "The advancement of international understanding, good will and peace through a world fellowship of business and professional people united in the ideal of service." This cornerstone has been recognized by the Rotary Club of Traverse City for many years, and there is a growing awareness of the need to expand our role and responsibilities worldwide. Our activities involving international outreach have included a number of very special programs.

Rotary Youth Exchange

Rotary Youth Exchange is one of Rotary International's most popular programs to promote international understanding and develop lifelong friendships. It began in 1927 with the Rotary Club of Nice, France. In 1939 an extensive Youth Exchange was created between California and Latin America. Since then the program has expanded around the world. In recent years more than 7,000 young people have participated annually in Rotary-sponsored exchange programs. Traverse City Rotary Club's Youth Exchange Program started in about 1972. It is estimated that we have hosted more than 75 students and sent over 100 of our students to countries around the world. Students inbound or returning from other countries and our outbound students, before traveling abroad, participate in extensive conferences, learning about U.S. diplomacy, foreign policy and current world events in preparation for their student Exchanges.

An extensive interviewing process begins as soon as school starts each year to choose the Traverse City students who will represent us abroad the following year. Typically, sophomore students are chosen to spend their junior year abroad. Inbound students who have just returned from the Exchange the previous school year actively participate in interviewing and selecting the next Exchange students.

Generally two foreign students arrive in Traverse City in August for a stay of about 11 months. A third student arrives in January and is also here for about 11 months. Each student stays with three different families, spending about 3-1/2 months with each one. This provides the students with the experience of living with several families. These Exchange students attend Rotary luncheons once a month, participate in the Rotary Show, and attend three District Conferences during the year. At the annual Christmas Party for Rotarians and their spouses, the students often give a short biography of themselves and explain how the holidays are celebrated in their own countries.

The values of Youth Exchange are experienced not only by the high school-age students involved, but also by the host families, sponsoring clubs, receiving high schools and the entire community. Youth Exchange participants usually provide their fellow students in their host schools with excellent opportunities to learn about customs, languages, traditions and family life in another country.

Rotary Youth Exchange students joining Rotarians and families at Christmas dinner.

Summer Austrian Youth Exchange

Since the early 1960s, Traverse City Rotary Club, along with the Linz, Austria Rotary Club, have exchanged students each summer. Because we are a Host Club, we are allowed to send two students to spend the summer with families in Austria. These students are usually juniors in high school, and it is recommended that they have some background in the German language. In turn, we host a group of approximately 12 to 15 young men and women ages 18 to 22 for approximately 10 days in the summer. This exchange is participated in by several clubs around the United States, all of which act as Host Clubs. The host families plan varied activities that include all the students and host families. Some families also take day trips to show the students some of the special features and beauty of our area. If a student has a particular interest, generally a Rotarian will step forward and help with finding a way to satisfy that interest.

The Austrian Youth Exchange is one of the most pleasant programs the Traverse City Rotary Club experiences. The students we host are bright, college-bound young men and women from Austria who speak fluent English and, in most instances, come from Rotary families in Austria. They become a member of the host family for the 10 days they are here, and they are very eager to learn the ways of America. Our Club members have discovered that through this unique program, many members have come to know each other better. It has also been possible to form many friendships in Austria with the parents of these students.

Group Study Exchange

Another very rewarding program in which Traverse City Rotary participates is the adult Group Study Exchange sponsored by the Rotary Foundation of Rotary International. Teams of non-Rotarian business and professional men and women, typically led by a Rotarian, visit each other's country for several weeks to study economic and cultural practices, as well as their own vocations or professions. The first exchange between Rotary Districts was between California and Japan, beginning in 1965. Since that time, it has been estimated that the Group Study Exchange has involved educational and cultural visits by approximately 37,000 business and professional men and women, serving on over 7,600 teams from more than 100 countries. The Rotary Foundation has provided more than $68 million in support of these exchanges, which provide the opportunity for paired Districts from diverse areas of the globe to send and receive study teams each year.

Men and women from Traverse City, both Rotarians and non-Rotarians, have participated in Group Study Exchanges in the Philippines, South Africa, Ecuador, Korea, Spain, Sweden, England, Australia, West Indies and Indonesia. Traverse City has also hosted foreign teams, beginning in 1974, from Denmark, Germany, India, Australia/New Guinea, Scotland,

Netherlands and France. These exchange participants, both outbound and inbound, have visited governmental agencies, businesses large and small, educational institutions and professional work places in distant lands, not only learning a great deal about how businesses and cultural activities are conducted elsewhere, but also imparting valuable knowledge from their home districts. While visiting abroad, team members are hosted in the homes of local Rotarians, again establishing close and long-lasting personal friendships and exchanges of ideas.

Rotary Foundation–International Aid Programs

The mission of the Rotary Foundation of Rotary International is to support the efforts of Rotary International in achieving world understanding and peace through international humanitarian, educational and cultural programs, including the Group Study Exchange described above. In the humanitarian category, Rotary International and the Rotary Foundation determined in 1985 to establish as one of its highest priorities joining in a massive effort to immunize all children of the world against poliomyelitis, commonly known as polio. The program was named "PolioPlus," a global effort to protect children not only from polio, but also from five other deadly diseases present in many areas of the world—thus the "Plus" in the program's name. The original goal of Rotary International and Rotary Foundation was to raise $120 million for this effort. By 1988, Rotarians throughout the world had raised more than $219 million, and as of June 1999, more than $340 million. Grants for such immunization have been made to over 100 countries, and in 1999 only 50 of those countries remained polio-endemic. Working in partnership with many national governments, the World and Pan American Health Organizations, UNICEF and others, Rotary International is hoping to celebrate a polio-free world in its own 100th anniversary year, 2005. The Rotary Club of Traverse City mounted a major pledge drive of its members in the late 1980s, and at the end of that pledge drive on June 30, 1989 individual members, with matching grants from Rotary Charities, provided over $302,000 to the PolioPlus campaign, representing the highest per capita giving for that cause of any Rotary Club, at least in the U.S.A., if not worldwide.

Other Rotary Foundation and Rotary International projects supported by Traverse City Rotary include the Malaysian Sunshine Orphans' Camp; building improvements for a tuberculosis sanatorium in India; providing cash contributions and medical equipment for the Trelawny, Jamaica medical clinic; a water well in India; $4000 for a greenhouse in Bonaire in the Netherlands Antilles to provide work programs for adult mentally handicapped persons and thereby provide funds for their related programs; support of all District 6290 International Aid programs through the years; and cash contributions by members each year to the Rotary Foundation in the form of Paul Harris Fellow Awards, some of which are given by the Club to honor local non-Rotarian citizens who personify service above self in their daily lives and careers.

Another recent project undertaken by the Club has been support of the Bali Blood Center in Indonesia, a project of the Bali Rotary Club. Members of the Traverse City Club individually pledged $10,000 for the blood center, matched by $10,000 from Rotary Charities, which total was applied to the construction of the Center. An additional $11,000 was obtained from District 6290 funds through a grant application spearheaded by leadership from our Club, which amount was matched by the Rotary Foundation, to purchase two bloodmobiles. The Bali Blood Center serves 7-1/2 million people.

Finally, our Club has undertaken support of the Rotary Club of Denpasar, also on the Island of Bali, to provide tuition, books, supplies, meals, uniforms, shoes and daily vitamins for children who would otherwise not be able to attend any school, since a public school is not available. The project, called "Help the Children," allows each child to obtain an education and better health at a cost of only $60 per year, so every contribution has major impact. Contributions from our individual members, with resulting matching monies from our district and the Rotary Foundation, will enable over 320 children to attend the school.

OTHER ROTARY SERVICE PROJECTS

STRIVE Scholarship Program

Other projects involving Rotarians have had a far-reaching impact upon our greater community for many years. One of the more recent is the STRIVE Program, which is a scholarship opportunity for high school seniors. Begun in 1995, the program is a partnership among the Traverse City Rotary Club, Traverse City Central High School, Traverse City West High School, St. Francis High School and Northwestern Michigan College. Students who have struggled academically are challenged to improve their grade point average during their senior year, and are also given the opportunity to have a Rotary member as a personal mentor. In order to qualify for a college scholarship, the students must maintain a good attitude, improve their grade point average and have a 95 per cent attendance level in school. In other words, they must succeed in the three Λ's: Attitude, Academics and Attendance. The funding comes from Rotary Club activities and member gifts. The program has proven highly successful, as 42 students thus far have received such scholarships to Northwestern Michigan College, totaling more than $64,000 since 1995, for an average of over $1500 per student.

Birthday Fund Scholarships

Scholarship aid for Northwestern Michigan College students has been provided by the Rotary Club since 1952. One means of supporting these scholarships has been individual members being "hit up" on their respective birthdays, when they are requested by the Club to contribute whatever amount of money they choose to the "Birthday Fund." A review of the archives reveals at least 55 students received scholarships through 1995, and many others received student loans from a fund to which the Club contributed in the earlier years. Beginning in 1995 the Birthday Fund contributions have been added to the STRIVE scholarships.

Christmas Basket Program

Each year the Club sponsors a project to help needy families have a more joyous Christmas by providing food, clothing, toys for the children and occasionally funds to meet other special needs. Shortly after Thanksgiving each year, members are requested to donate money to the project. The receiving families are selected from nominees submitted by local Social Service units, churches, schools and the Rotary membership. Family assignments are made primarily to new members, although the full membership is invited to participate. The Rotarian is given a share of the total collections and is instructed to contact the selected family to determine its specific needs. The Rotarian and his/her own family then do the shopping, wrap the items where appropriate and make a personal visit to the needy family to deliver the Christmas basket. In 1982, contributions totaled $1835, which was contributed to provide aid to 10 families. Enthusiasm and commitment has grown significantly over the years, and now approximately $5,000 is raised each year, providing a much merrier Christmas to 24 families, including 72 children, in 1999.

Northwestern Michigan College Barbecue

The Northwestern Michigan College Barbecue was started in 1956 by local grocery store entrepreneur, Gerald Oleson (a Kiwanian who was made an honorary Rotarian for his matchless community support in so many ways). The Barbecue was established as a fund-raiser for the then new community college, which had been established five years earlier. Mr. Oleson donated the food, and community volunteers provided the labor for this much anticipated event in May on the college campus, which feeds up to 12,000 people or more each year. Along with other service groups, Rotary Club members from the beginning were major participants in this exciting event, showing up at dawn on the Sunday of the Barbeque to stoke up the grills and begin cooking the delicious barbequed buffalo burgers from morning until early evening, in two-hour shifts. Over $1 million has been raised over the years, and the proceeds have been used to fund over 120 special college projects. Rotary has been proud to lend its support to this enjoyable gathering of community members and visitors to our area every year for over 40 years.

Grilling buffalo burgers at Northwestern Michigan College Barbecue.

Grand Traverse Pavilions Renaissance Fair

A similar but more recently created event is the Renaissance Fair held in August every year on the beautiful grounds and new facilities of the Grand Traverse Pavilions (formerly known as the Grand Traverse County Medical Care Facility). This has become a major fund-raiser for the region's, if not the country's, premier intergenerational health care and residential community. Commencing in 1992, the Fair attracts approximately 3,000 visitors each year, who are treated to traditional food, costumes, games and entertainment of the Renaissance Period. Rotarians, along with other enthusiastic community volunteers, work in various activities at the Fair, including the grilling of chicken and turkey legs (preparation and consumption of food appear to be special talents of our Club). Proceeds from the Fair benefit the outstanding programs and facilities of the Grand Traverse Pavilions, which is the only such center in the state having a complex that features child care, adult day and overnight respite care, long-term skilled nursing and assisted living programs.

Youth Recognition

Rotary as an organization, as well as individual members, participate in many other activities, particularly involving youth. One additional example is honoring outstanding students from the area high schools, two of whom are selected each week by school administrators to visit with Rotary at its regular Tuesday noon meetings. This is a means of recognizing the outstanding achievements of the young people of our area, as well as introducing them to Rotary members, activities and antics. Hundreds of students have made such visits over many years, helping to maintain a tangible connection between Rotary and the promise of the future.

To Whom Much Is Given

This is the basic story of the Traverse City Rotary Club during the 20th Century. It is truly a story with a happy ending, that should really never end. It exists because Paul Harris, a visionary man in Chicago, organized a small group of diverse business friends to meet regularly. He gave them a precept, "Service Above Self," which is followed worldwide by more than a million Rotarians today. Because the Traverse City Rotary Club followed that precept in securing land for youth activities, and because that land sits on top of oil and gas reserves, this area has experienced a bounty it might never have known.

Luke 12, verse 48 reads: "For unto whomsoever much is given, of him shall be much required . . ." What we have been given refers not only to monetary wealth, but also to our upbringing, talents, intellect, education, position and other resources, tangible and intangible, with which we are blessed. Since the 1920's Traverse City Rotarians, like so many other individuals and service organizations, have responded as required, by recognizing that we need to share our life gifts with those in greater need. This was a strong belief long before mineral revenues were available.

One of these days the oil and gas wells will dry up. But

thanks to the foresight of some very dedicated people, the Grand Traverse area will continue to benefit well into the far distant future, because of the perpetual endowment that was formed and because future Rotarians will continue to give of themselves.

So, conceivably the Traverse City Rotary Club is one of the richest Rotary Clubs in the world—not necessarily financially, because the oil and gas revenue does not belong to or go directly to the Club. Its richness is in its cohesive membership, and in its ability to implement ideals of Rotary International and to promote its own civic, cultural and moral values. If the Club's members of the present and future can match the work and dedication of those members of the past, it will certainly continue to be a club of which Rotary International and others can be proud—a club giving service to the community and the world.

APPENDIX A

Charter Members of the Rotary Club of Traverse City (1920)

Members	Classification
George R. Becker	Real Estate
Milton B. Bryant	Autos–Passenger
Rev. Demas Cochlin	Clergy
John O. Duncan	Attorney
Charles J. Ebner	Printer
Clarence L. Greilick	Furniture
Dr. Guy M. Johnson	Hospitals
George K. Kilbourne	Abstractor
Frederick P. Lawton	Surgeon
Augustus J. Maynard	Banker
William M. McCool	Ice Cream Manufacture
James T. Milliken	Retail Dry Goods
Howard A. Musselman	Groceries, Wholesale
John L. Novak	Agricultural Instruments
William W. Parr	Retail Lumber
Glen W. Power	Life Insurance
Wallace G. Rath	Motors
John R. Santo	Fire Insurance
Dr. Shiloh S. Smith	Dentist
Ed L. Soderberg	Reed Furniture Manufacture
Lewis Stocking	Insurance, Miscellaneous
John C. Straub	Confectioner
Leon F. Titus	Agriculture, Farming
Charles P. Zapf	Fruit

First Officers and Directors

James T. Milliken	President & Director
John O. Duncan	Vice President & Director
Leon F. Titus	Secretary-Treasurer & Director
Rev. Demas Cochlin	Director
Dr. Guy M. Johnson	Director
Frederick P. Lawton	Director
William M. McCool	Director

APPENDIX B

Club Presidents - Rotary Club of Traverse City.

James T. Milliken	1920-22	James J. Beckett	1961-62
Arthur Rowley	1922-23	A. Kent Schafer	1962-63
Clarence L. Greilick	1923-24	John W. Rennie	1963-64
Guy M. Johnson	1924-25	Jerry W. McCarthy	1964-65
Glenn W. Power	1925-26	Bruce Needham	1965-66
Charles Poor	1926-27	Jackson Bensley	1966-67
Fred H. Pratt	1927-28	John R. Anderson	1967-68
Bert H. Comstock	1928-29	G. Curt Alward	1968-69
Hugh J. Johnston	1929-30	Winton Klotzbach	1969-70
Harry L. Weaver	1930-31	Frank L. Stulen, PDG	1970-71
Arthur P. Eva	1931-32	Austin Van Stratt	1971-72
William J. Hobbs	1932-33	Kenneth Lindsey	1972-73
Gordon C. Pharo	1933-34	David E. Pearce	1973-74
Lars Hockstad	1935-36	Kenneth C. Taylor	1974-75
Austin C. Batdorff	1936-37	Preston N. Tanis	1975-76
Ben L. Taylor	1936-37	William F. Kildee	1976-77
Donald C. Roxburgh	1937-38	Joseph G. Groszek	1977-78
Frank Sleder	1938-39	William McCort	1978-79
Robert B. Murchie	1939-40	Joseph J. Muha	1979-80
Gerhard Harsch	1940-41	Robert W. Dopke	1980-81
Kenneth W. Tinker	1941-42	John C. Bay	1981-82
Harold E. Johnson	1942-43	Roger E. Jacobi	1982-83
Douglas E. Linder	1943-44	Don A. Good	1983-84
Willis Heidbreder	1944-45	Maurie Dennis	1984-85
Arthur S. Huey, PDG	1945-46	Kenneth Musson	1985-86
George Olmstead	1946-47	Peter M. Strom	1986-87
G. Karl Fisher	1947-48	Jim VanEenenaam	1987-88
Harold Jordon	1948-49	George McManus, Jr.	1988-89
John Minnema	1949-50	Leo J. Hughes	1989-90
William F. Martinek	1950-51	Gary L. Columbus	1990-91
Frank Power	1951-52	John C. Burns	1991-92
Paul Wilson	1952-53	Donald C. Fraser	1992-93
Erich J. Sleder	1953-54	Jack Stegenga	1993-94
John P. Freethy	1953-54	Paul Mocere	1994-95
Harford Field	1955-56	Daniel A. Jonkhoff	1995-96
Mark Osterlin	1956-57	K. Ross Childs	1996-97
Paul Garthe	1957-58	Donald P. Piche	1997-98
Hal Votey	1958-59	Ralph Soffredine	1998-99
Bob D. Hilty	1959-60	Thomas E. Gartland	1999-2000
Ben I. Taylor	1960-61	William R. Shoskey	2000-2001

APPENDIX C

Past District Governors - District 6290

Arthur S. Huey	1953-54
R. Graham Keevil	1969-70
John R. Broadfoot (Dist. 631)	1979-80
Frank L. Stulen	1982-83
Franklin G. Sisson	1987-88

Club Secretaries - Rotary Club of Traverse City

Leon F. Titus	1920-21
Demas Cochlin	1921-23
Charles Sherwood	1923-25
William E. Votruba	1925-26
Sprague Pratt	1926-32
Clair B. Curtis	1932-47
Harold E. Johnson	1947-48
Hugh J. Johnston	1948-49
William F. Martinek	1949-50
Karl Fisher	1950-55
R. Graham Keevil	1955-77
James H. Sargent	1981-91
William H. McCort	1991-92
Robert D. Yeiter	1992-

APPENDIX D
Rotary Charities Presidents

Frank H. Power/Bob D. Hilty 1977-78
Bob D. Hilty 1978-82
William K. Kildee 1982-83
John R. Anderson 1983-84
Winton Klotzbach 1984-86
Kenneth C. Taylor 1986-88
W. Bruce Rogers 1988-90
Leon B. Michael 1990-92
Jerry Meyers 1992-93
Norman Kline 1993-94
Joseph J. Muha 1994-96
John C. Bay 1996-98
Laurence P. Skendzel/Robert A. Dean 1998-99
Robert A. Dean 1999-00
John A. Yeager 2000-01

Rotary Camps & Services Presidents

Frank H. Power 1976-77
Frank H. Power/Bob D. Hilty 1977-78
Bob D. Hilty 1978-82
William F. Kildee 1982-83
John R. Anderson 1983-84
Winton Klotzbach 1984-86
Kenneth C. Taylor 1986-87
Roger E. Jacobi 1987-89
Roger E. Jacobi/Kenneth A. Lindsay 1989-90
Donald A. Good 1990-92
H. Wendell Johnson 1992-94
Kenneth H. Musson 1994-95
Donald L. Fraser 1995-97
John R. Williams 1997-99
James D. Elkins 1999-00
George M. Powell 2000-01

APPENDIX E

PHOTOGRAPHS OF REPRESENTATIVE PROJECTS SUPPORTED BY ROTARY GRANTS

Watervale Peninsula south of Frankfort in Benzie County, where two conservation easements on more than two miles of Lake Michigan and Lower Herring Lake are held by the Grand Traverse Regional Land Conservancy, with major Rotary Camps' negotiation and support.

Mancelona Health Care Clinic in Antrim County.

The new Traverse Area District Library serves as a resource center for the entire region.

Glen Arbor Township Park tennis courts in Leelanau County.

An Elmwood Township section of the T.A.R.T Trails, Inc., a regional recreational trails organization incubated by Rotary.

Bleachers for Bellaire Schools athletic field in Antrim County.

140-bed dormitory at Twin Lakes 4-H Camp, serving 4-H'ers from the five-county area.

Suttons Bay Library in Leelanau County.

New addition to Benzie Area Historical Museum in Benzonia.

Traverse City West Junior High School athletic field—1990.

Alden railroad museum and park in Antrim County.

Rotary was there to purchase the first thermal imaging camera for use by the Traverse City Fire Department.

"Between the Fences" project for Thirlby/Running Field in Traverse City.

Glen Lake Township Library in Leelanau County.

Detroit Red Wings legend, Gordie Howe, and his wife Colleen, at the dedication ceremonies for the Howe Arena, supported by a Rotary grant to the Grand Traverse County Parks and Recreation Department.

President Roger Jacobi checking out new school bus provided for Interlochen Center for the Arts in 1987.

APPENDIX F
PHOTOGRAPHS FROM PAST ROTARY SHOWS

The Rotary Chorus in traditional black-face, which ended in 1960's in response to racial sensitivity.

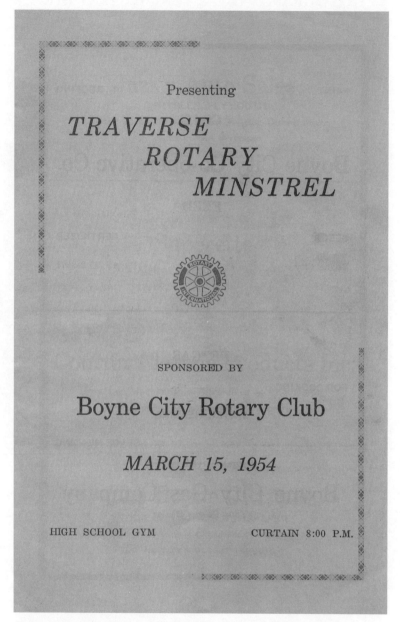

Presenting

TRAVERSE
ROTARY
MINSTREL

SPONSORED BY

Boyne City Rotary Club

MARCH 15, 1954

HIGH SCHOOL GYM   CURTAIN 8:00 P.M.

Program cover from 1954 Rotary Show "on the road" in Boyne City.

Pit Band blowing off steam at Louie Sleder's Tavern after 1961 Show.

Kiwanians unsuccessfully picket State Theatre during 1964 Show.

Endman Dave Pearce leads chorus under pipes in basement of State Theatre toward stage in 1965 Rotary Show.

World Premier of the "Flying Walnettos" - 1969.

Pit Band of 1969

Bicentennial Rotary Chorus in 1976 (bass section).

Bill Kildee and Walt Campbell, well-known in Traverse City as the Rotary Minstrels' feature act "Willy and Wally," made the trip down to Washington, D.C. to help give Griffin the raspberries. Officials for the event even termed the Griffin roast as one of the best ever.

Griffin gets into the spirit of the event and puts a strangle hold on his old Senate friend Hubert H. Humphrey (D., Minn). A couple of Saints and Sinners officials stand in the background. No women – except the Senator's wife – were allowed to attend which prompted a protest from Griffin's female office staff. Reports have it that some of the "roasting" was somewhat on the raunchy side.

35th Anniversary Rotary Show at old State Theatre in 1977.

Austrian exchange student, Gina Chemelar, expertly applies make-up to Bob Dopke for 40th Rotary Show (1982).

Father Mularkey's (Leo Hughes) 1986 Annual Parish Report.

This "collage" reminiscence was part of the Golden Anniversary Rotary Show Program in 1992.

Dedication

This year's 50th Anniversary Minstrel Show is dedicated to all Traverse City Rotarians, past and present, who have given of themselves through the years so that our community might be a better place to live. Rotarians, through this Minstrel Show have not only provided us all an opportunity to laugh at ourselves but also helped to provide generous "Good Works" funds that have touched many lives.

A sampling of some of these "Minstrels" are pictured in a "reminiscence collage" of previous Minstrel Show snapshots below and on the next few pages."

Rotary Minstrel Show Reminiscence

▲ 1951 Jack Bensley, Bill Kildee, & Wally Campbell

▲ 1947 Interlocutor Doug Linder

1981 George Worden, ► Tom Bensley & George McManus

Rotary Minstrel Show Reminiscence

1965 News Report ▶
Jack Bensley, &
Dave Pearce

1982 Jack Stegenga
▼

1983 Jerry Meyer, Leo Hughes ▶
& Ben Taylor

▲ 1977 "Mule Train" Bill Kildee

▲ Jon Petersen, **Music Director**
for many years.

Rotary Minstrel Show Reminiscence

◄ The Fudgies

1979
Jerry Meyer,
Bill Kildee,
and Leo Hughes ▼

◄ "The Drunk"
Jerry Hager

"The Doorman"
Eric Sleder ►

◄ 1978
Jack Keane & Paul Mocere

Cover of 1992 50th Anniversary Rotary Show program.

Rotary Anns (wives) in 1992 decided to have their own Rotary Show act.

Program cover from year 2000 Rotary Show.

POETIC EPILOGUE

This concluding segment of our book represents the writing of Frank Sisson, our beloved poet laureate and humorist. Frank was in television and radio broadcasting for many years in the Detroit area where he also served as President of the Detroit Rotary Club. Since joining the Traverse City Club in 1984, Frank has served as our District Governor in 1987-88. He has also regaled Rotarians and other audiences for years with presentations of his original poems, as well as dramatic presentations of such classics as "Old Mother Hubbard" and musical variety acts at the annual Rotary Show.

Frank was also of major assistance in the production of this book and is a member of the Book Committee.

Following are a dozen examples (since Frank advised us that they would be cheaper by the dozen) of his poetry relating to Rotary and individual Rotarians about whom he writes in the weekly Rotary Bulletin. His self-deprecating humor reflects the humility of this very talented Rotarian.

Joyce Kilmer thought he'd never see
A poem lovely as a tree,
But then, in all humility,
He never saw one writ by me.

The Bare Facts

After enduring what I've been called,
(There's little I've been spared)
I find that I'm not really bald,
I'm follicly impaired!

Golden Years

I well recall Your Hit Parade,
Lum and Abner, Vic and Sade.
Mumblety-peg and Myrna Loy,
Jackie Cooper as a boy,
Ice cards at the window pane,
Using coal to fuel a train,
Maggie, who was Jiggs' spouse,
Doctors coming to the house,
Fireflies stuffed in Mason jars,
Cobbled streets and trolley cars,
Herbert Hoover, Prohibition,
Thurston, what a great magician!
Within my cell depleted brain,
It's stuff like this that I retain,
Which makes me wonder why it's so,
I can't <u>forget</u> the long ago,
But can't <u>remember</u>, come what may,
Those things I planned to do today!

To Whom Much Is Given

Park Place Hotel Progress Report given by Rotary Center to
Rotary Charities, August 28, 1990

Oh, Rotary Charities gave us a job
and three and a half million bucks,
And told us the Park Place was ours to redo,
and we'd better redo it deluxe!

"It might take a bit of repairing," they said,
"some patching, some caulking, some paint,
But with all of that dough you should make the place glow,
and turn it to something it ain't!"

So, with Arthur G. Elliott leading the charge,
the Center Board sprang to the fore,
Deserting their wives and devoting their lives
to discovering how to restore

This lovely old edifice, three score in age,
a gal who remembers the day
When she was the pride of the city's downtown,
the jewel adorning the bay.

So work was begun and surprises were rife
as Arthur began writing checks,
"Hey!" Charities cried, "Make the hotel an anchor,
but don't tie its rope 'round our necks!"

But back came the board of the Rotary Center,
extending a hat in its hand,
And they said that for just about four million more,
the Park Place could really look grand.

And Charities said, "You sound quite convincing,"
and went once again to the vault,
With stern admonitions that further surprises
might bring the whole thing to a halt.

But now that the drawings and plans are completed,
and workers are ready to start,
The visions of Park Place remodeled are forming,
and adding a beat to the heart.

And we dream of a downtown that's booming,
alive in its beauty and power,
With the city's Rotarians proudly proclaiming
that this is its finest hour!

To Whom Much Is Given

(Adam McClay, orthopedic surgeon)

You can travel the length of the Appian Way,
Read writings by Edna St. Vincent Millay,
Drop a jigger of rum in your café au lait,
While enjoying the scenery of old Monterey;
You can go for a spin in your new Chevrolet,
Buy a priceless old painting by Edouard Monet,
But such things are nothing, I've heard people say,
Compared to an evening with Adam McClay!

(Frank Stulen, world renowned engineer and inventor,
Past Club President and Past District Governor)

Regardless your status or rank,
This advice you can take to the bank,
Be sure you keep cool in
Discussions with Stulen,
Cause Stulen is perfectly Frank!

94

(Major Art Huey, Past Club President, Past District Governor, and as of May 23, 1999, a Traverse City Rotarian for sixty years!)

While it's hard to believe it's quite true, he
Joined the club before Truman beat Dewey;
Shortly after sliced bread,
Before Zsa Zsa first wed,
That's how long we've enjoyed Arthur Huey!

*(Roger Jacobi, retired President Interlochen
Center for the Arts, Past Club President)*

You can search from Rangoon to Nairobi,
Or head north where the sleet and the snow be,
You can go from the Soo
Down to Kalamazoo,
But you'll not find another Jacobi!

To Whom Much Is Given

(Paul Morris, professional choral director, development director/fund raiser, and leader of the Rotary Chorus)

Our voices singly leave much to desire,
No matter how we struggle and perspire,
But together, led by Morris, we're the Hallelujah Chorus,
Of the awesome Mormon Tabernacle Choir!

(Hal "Red" Johnson, retired Commander/Conductor Air Force Bands, and pianist for the Club)

Tuesday's a "Red" letter day!

The reason why Tuesday deserves a red letter,
Most ev'ry Rotarian agrees,
Is the food at the Park Place just seems to taste better
When Johnson starts ticklin' those keys.

So, here's to the guy who can make pulses pump,
With a talent that no one can question,
He's not only able to make the joint jump,
He gets rid of our (burp) indigestion!

*(Leon Olewinski, hospital executive
and Rotary Charities Trustee)*

Everybody Sing!

Tune: Supercalifragilisticexpyalidocious!

SupercalifragilisticLEONOLEWINSKI,
A word that's so much fun to say,
I cannot help but grinsky.
I say it and replay it 'til my poor head starts to spinsky,
SupercalifragilisticLEONOLEWINSKI!

Bump diddle dee dum bump bump bump

SupercalifragilisticLEONOLEWINSKI,
So musical and danceable,
I kick up both my shinski,
And minuet and pirouette just like that guy Nijinsky,
SupercalifragilisticLEONOLEWINSKI!

To Whom Much Is Given

*(Dan Jonkhoff, friendly undertaker
and Past Club President)*

While I'm aging a bit and have just a suggestion
Of memory loss plus a mild indigestion,
I don't mind revealing just how I am feeling,
But hate it when Jonkhoff keeps asking the question!

While his work place might make you feel queasy,
He's so affable, cheerful and breezy,
That you know from the start
Dan's a man of good heart,
And a guy who will let your down easy!

Franklin G. Sisson

To obtain additional copies of this book,
please send $20.00 to:

Rotary Charities of Traverse City, Inc.
115 Park Street
Traverse City, MI 49684

or call
231-941-4010